Mastering the Pain

Jonas Gilham

Copyright © 2020 Jonas Gilham

All rights reserved. No part of this book may be reproduced or transmitted or stored in any form or by any means, electronic or mechanical, including photocopying, recording, or any information storage and retrieval, without permission in writing from the Copyright owner.

PART I: My Youth 1

- ❒ Governed By a Different Standard 3
- ❒ He Dared Me To 6
- ❒ Miner Playground 7
- ❒ P's and Q's 9
- ❒ Reflection 11

PART II: The Struggle 13

- ❒ Slowly Fading Away 15
- ❒ A Dropped Call? 17
- ❒ It's Such a Cold, Damp Day 19
- ❒ A Song From A Caged Bird 21
- ❒ Unconscious Tears 23
- ❒ Expect the Unexpected 24

PART III: Reflections/Introspection 25

- ❒ Locked Up 27
- ❒ She 29
- ❒ Silence is Golden 31
- ❒ My Homies, R.I.P. 32
- ❒ Dignity 34
- ❒ Tribal Ties 35
- ❒ Empathy 36
- ❒ Crayons 38
- ❒ Redemption 40
- ❒ Learning 41

- ❐ Just The Simple Things..42
- ❐ Observe, Don't Absorb 45
- ❐ Royalty Redeemed 49
- ❐ Mastering the Pain 51

PART IV: The Light...53

- ❐ My Roots...55
- ❐ Beauty in my Blackness...57
- ❐ My World..59
- ❐ Justice for Trayvon - The George Zimmerman Trial 61
- ❐ The Verdict...66
- ❐ Where Do We Go From Here? - A Tribute for Young Trayvon.............70
- ❐ What is Dead May Never Die..76
- ❐ So Disrespectful...78
- ❐ Respect My "G"...81
- ❐ Death Before Dishonor 82
- ❐ We Need to Celebrate Our Achievements More! 84
- ❐ The Journey..86
- ❐ Victorious...88
- ❐ Destiny Is Here 90

PART V: Love...91

- ❐ Big Homie...93
- ❐ A Vision 95
- ❐ Uncharted Waters..97
- ❐ In Her Eyes 99
- ❐ A Familiar Soul..101
- ❐ Women 103
- ❐ Hope..104
- ❐ Missin' You For Debo..105
- ❐ Her Embrace 107
- ❐ About the Author 109

Introduction

I wrote this poetry and personal narrative collection throughout the course of my incarceration. I've been in prison since I was 16 years-old. I am now 33. This book is an effort to understand the influences that led me to this stage in my life; a way for me to cope with the hardships and trauma of being incarcerated for such a long period of time; and a way to process and make sense out of the chaos and confusion that consumed me in my youth. It is me battling my demons, grasping for some glimmer of hope when all hope seemed to be lost. It is me begging for forgiveness from those whom I have harmed, and granting it to those who have harmed me. It is me searching for my own beauty and humanity, and the beauty and humanity of the world. This book is me being vulnerable, seeking connection. It is me striving for a karmic balance through my pen and pad. Journey with me as I embark on my road to redemption. I hope that you come out on the other end as encouraged and inspired as I am today.

PART I
My Youth

Governed By a Different Standard

Early lessons taught us to demand respect, get money, and earn your keep amongst men. Weakness is not tolerated in any way, shape, form or fashion. If he has something in his possession, something he hasn't proven he has the right to have, then it's your right to take it. As a matter of fact, you're almost obligated to do so; either by intimidation or brute force. By any means necessary. In a war zone where territory equals more money, every hood is looking to advance. Having a coward handling or governing any type of business ventures, or otherwise lucrative enterprise, would scar the reputation of the hood and jeopardize its security. In fact, the very presence of a "sucka" amongst thoroughbreds is unheard of. It upsets the natural order of things. There's no room for perpetrating. Sooner or later, you get exposed for what you really are. All it takes is for the right situation to present itself. Often times, that situation presents itself in the form of another thoroughbred challenging your status, calling you out for whatever his reasons may be. Your response must be that of pure and unfiltered aggression. You have to correct the situation in whatever way is called for. Everything depends on it. Nearly all that you've earned from the work you've put in can be renewed or revoked within those crucial moments. No hesitation, all systems are go.

Certain words or accusations are automatic grounds for physical violence. "You a bitch!", "Suck my dick!", or "You a rat!" These are probably the three that call for the most swift and severe reaction. Anything less and those statements might as well be true because in the minds of everyone else, they certainly will be. There is no room for thought; just action.

My Youth

There are six of us on the block, late at night, on the grind. All of us are strapped with guns. The hood that we're beefin' with comes through and does a drive by. Four of us buzz, forcing them to retreat. No one on our side is hit, but those remaining two dudes are automatically demoted to a lesser status and won't be allowed to hustle on the block anymore. They've shown that they can't hold it down. They froze. They stopped, and there's zero tolerance for that. You have to be born with it, torn from this fabric, a bird of this feather.

There is a lot of bloodshed, a lot of death. You can lose your life because you misjudged the caliber of a man and decided to try him, or simply because you were in a situation and you hesitated. Your street intuition must be strong in order to move smoothly within a world where every step is critical. You must be as fluid as water, or you won't last very long. Whatever your motivation is; hustling, robbing, extortion, murder for hire, pimpin', it doesn't matter. You gotta be able to hold it down. In order to really rise above and last longer than the rest, there's got to be a balance of intelligence and an attitude of, "I sincerely don't give a fuck." It's absolutely necessary to have a certain degree of recklessness, but be intelligent and self-controlled enough to know when and how to turn it on and off. Recklessness, in over-drive, will almost always lead to an early death. Someone will kill you. Survival of the fittest is the order of each day. You quickly learn that nobody's gonna give you anything. Nothing comes free. When your stomach is grumbling and there's nothing but lint in your pockets, you go take what you need. When you're tired of getting robbed, beaten up and ridiculed on a daily basis, you're forced to either go hard and become an extremely violent individual in order to reset your tone, or continue to travel the trail of a coward. The environment molds you quickly.

Time goes by and before you know it, you've been putting in work for a while, maintaining, and a dramatic change occurs in your life. You get locked up. You have to serve eight on a ten-year bid. You go from being a free man to an incarcerated one. Then the dynamics change. They become more intense. If you're one who has just been getting by because you have five older brothers and/or ten cousins who are official, or you have that "my man and 'em" attitude, you're in for a very rude awakening. You come here alone, your brothers, cousins and "homies" are nowhere around to help. Your reputation from the streets will only carry you so far. Everyone around you has a reputation from the streets on some level.

Governed By a Different Standard

The dynamics of this situation change on a few different fronts. When you're stripped of everything dear to you, you try to hold on to the little bit of dignity and pride you have left. In turn, the smallest things, stuff that once upon a time didn't mean much of anything becomes of the utmost importance. Emotions run high in prison due to the stress and feelings of powerlessness and isolation. Mix this with the sheer determination to preserve any amount of self-respect you have left, and a situation as simple as you accidentally bumping into someone without saying excuse me, or cutting in the line at chow time, or changing the T.V. while someone is watching it, can become a matter of life or death. If you find yourself in a similar situation and aren't intelligent enough to handle it accordingly, then there's a strong chance that man, who you've so blatantly disrespected, will come and try to kill you. You may have been a gun buster in the street, but anybody can shoot a gun. There are no pistols behind the wall. The weapon in prison is the knife! Every once in a while, you may see someone throw the lock in the sock and beat someone with it, or someone might get their hands on a random object like a mop stick or a fire extinguisher, but the knife is what separates the boys from the men.

Stabbing a person is a completely different experience. With a gun, you can hit your man from long distance and be on the move before the body hits the ground. With a knife, you're forced to be up close and personal, forced to look that man in his eyes, forced to push the knife into this man's body and feel it penetrate through his flesh, multiple times, sometimes hitting bones. Whatever the situation, whether you're right or wrong, you have to be ready. You've graduated. The streets were like high school academics, and in the pen, you have to perform on a collegiate level. Welcome to undergrad! For some, the transition is a relatively smooth one and for others, an extremely rough and bumpy experience. For some, it's just a complete and epic fail. If you have no heart and no balls, then you have nothing coming but a whole lot of misery. When your mindset and environment is governed by this standard, at no point can you afford to have a weak constitution. You can never break, bend or fold. That's when you are as thorough as they come.

These are the standards that raised me, the rules that shaped my youth, the mindset that limited my potential in so many ways. I am and have always been so much more.

He Dared Me To...

He dared me to do it. Those were my foolish days, so I did it. I was younger and more easily manipulated. So I did it. I hit him right across his wood. He hit the ground and when he was in the process, I saw his eyes roll in the back of his head and blood was gushing from his nose. I was high off of a real strong chemical drug called *The Dippa'*.

I kicked and stomped on his head and didn't really care. Those were my younger, foolish days. We didn't even rob the dude. Now, I feel remorseful because I know it was wrong. Now, I have a better, clearer and positive aspect on life. No more wild or so-called *thug life*.

Miner Playground

In the early 2000's
All the young people from my block hung out at Miner Playground
Till one or two in the morning sometimes
Someone's stereo from home was blasting go-go
The boys were playing basketball
The girls were standing on the sideline
Rooting for their crush
Someone would start dancing
And then it was just a big party on the playground
Anytime I hear old BYB
I think of Miner Playground
Loud talking and laughter
Young boys and girls running back and forth
Between two sets of sliding boards and monkey bars
Flirting with each other
The smell of carry-out food mixing with weed smoke
On a mild summer night
Carefree times where the vibe was just good fun
Come fall, we were playing football on the field
Sometimes against guys from up the block

My Youth

Everyone bringing their equipment from Pop Warner going at it
Getting scolded, if one of our coaches happened to roll by and see us
If you took a really hard hit and just laid there in the grass
"He hurt, he hurt, he lying in the dirt!" everyone would chant
That usually made a kid get up and get back to the game
Unless of course, you were really hurt
Then we'd help you to the side of the field
On any given night
Miner Playground was so exciting
If you were from around my way
You had some fist fights on that playground
But we'd all be right back, out there, the very next day
Right back to the fun
If we stayed out past curfew
Our parents knew to come to the playground to find us
They'd identify their child
March him or her home
Giving a good tongue-lashing along the way
Miner Playground will forever be one of the best places of my childhood

P's and Q's

This life is full of struggles and lessons yet to discover
You slid in baby girl, but forgot to use a rubber?
You were that geeked; you just had to hit shawty raw?
Take my word for it, you've discovered a character flaw
I won't sit here and lie, see, I can't even front
Instant gratification is something we all want
But patience is a virtue, yeah, we're all still learning
Still, you woke up one morning and realized you were burning
Leaking a discharge that you've never seen
Well, for unprotected sex, the consequences can be mean
Stay on your P's and Q's
The situation got heated; your adrenaline hit its height
Your mind said "be cool"
Your nerves said "fight or take flight!"
His body language became threatening
You took that as a sign
You then became afraid, and pulled out your 9
He said, "Hold on! It ain't even like dat!"
Nervously, you turned around to leave but didn't consider one probable fact
He had his Glock 40 tucked, and shot you three times in the back

My Youth

In the hospital, you laid in critical condition, praying you would make it through
The lesson was harsh, but well received
If you draw your weapon, be prepared to use it too
Stay on your P's and Q's
You decide to get pissy drunk, where you can't even stand
All alone at the bar, no one lend a helping hand
You try to walk, but start to stumble, people look in awe
If you'd have drank more responsibly, perhaps then you'd have seen
Young boys approaching on your left, with larceny in their eyes
Both very young and kinda slight in size
You probably could've took them, but you were too tough
They took your watch, they took your money
And you don't know what happened to your shoe!
Now, you're all battered and bruised, don't know what to do
Hey, what can I say? Stay on your P's and Q's

Reflection

I'm sitting here up on my rack, wondering why?
Why I had to start thugging, why I had to buy
Into all the negativity surrounding me
Blind to the facts of life so I couldn't see
The deep depths of my mind was all into crime
I'm hood bangin', sellin' rocks
Yeah, I'm tryna' shine
I kept a Glock 17 across my waistline
And wouldn't hesitate to squeeze it if time came
I was so sick and tired of people testin' me
Everybody knew about my vulnerability
So I started perpetrating the big bad ass
I would pull my strap quick if you were talkin' trash
I used to get jumped a lot in my own hood
The friends that I thought I had were no good
I came to realize that everybody played for keeps
I had to think fast, had to stay up on my feet
The way I was livin', niggaz was always down to creep
And I wasn't gonna be the one that was gonna be put to sleep
So I talked fast, moved quick, tried not to slip

My Youth

Always making sure that I had a full clip
I hung with gangsta's and thugs, drug deala's and killaz
We were always on the block acting like some untamed gorillaz
I learned how to manipulate and intimidate
Avoiding any feelings that I thought I couldn't face
Violence was always a part of my daily life
I saw guys I looked up to beating up their own wife
Regular. No surprise. Just another day
To see someone getting' shot right in front of your face
Now I'm a lil' older and I see I need a change
I need to download a new system into my brain
I'm wiser now, I'm smarter and I see the light
It's 'bout time for this young man to start living right

PART II
The Struggle

Slowly Fading Away

I feel like I'm slowly fading
Like smoke into thin air
In constant search of a caring soul
But no one really cares
It's rare to find a genuine heart, truly sincere and kind
Especially when you end up in a predicament like mine
Snatched away from society at a very young age
With no guidance and no structure, I was living in a haze
But the past is done and gone, and my future seems bleak
I'm slowly fading away
Like a drunk when he drinks
I think this life is worth living
Sometimes it's hard to tell
It's like I was born into Satan's hands, then cast into hell
My potential is at a peak, where I'm beginning to see
But twenty years from now, who knows where I'll be
Still locked in a cell where my potential and worth is a "was"—a thing of the past
So vast my dreams and goals, things I aspire to achieve
It's a daily struggle for me to continue to believe
To believe that I could actually be more than a thug

The Struggle

To believe that a woman still wants to give me a kiss with her love
Still wants to see me smile and tell me I'm so cute
To see that I've blossomed into a wonderful man
Though I didn't have rich roots
Locked away like this, everyone seems to forget
I'm slowly fading away
Into a bottomless pit
Out of sight, out of mind, damn, it's a shame
Sometimes I wonder if certain people even remember my name
In a predicament like this, you become very aware
Before, ignorance was bliss and you don't know to be scared
I feel like I have so much to offer
But am I really even here?
Time waits for no one, and no one sees my tears
I'm ripe and ready for whatever
I'm 21 years young
Sometimes my soul feels 80, like it's almost done
I'm slowly fading away
Into a mist of confusion
Constantly wondering if my life is just an illusion

A Dropped Call?

Never one to jump to conclusions
I'm always willing to give a person the benefit of the doubt
Maybe they accidentally hung up
Perhaps their finger accidentally brushed up against the wrong button…
Yeah, that's probably what happened
I'll try again
Ring…ring…ring
Answering machine
Well, damn, I know I'm not lunchin'
I just heard them answer the phone a minute ago when I called
I'll try one more time
Ring…answering machine
Doesn't get any clearer than that, oh well.
Wonder what's for chow tonight?
Only if it were actually that simple
That would be great
But in reality, the rest of my day is defined by a storm of confusion
All of my doubts, fears and anxieties whirling around in my head
Like tree branches and back yard garbage cans in a hurricane
That big, bluish-black monster named Depression

The Struggle

Begins to creep and stalk me like a vulture in the desert
I'm fully aware of his big, ugly presence
He's as cold as ice
And the closer he gets, the more depleted I feel
I try to fight him, but I'm totally disarmed
And he continues to consume me whole, slowly but surely
All of a sudden, I feel exhausted and I have to lay down to sleep
I awake in the calm of my storm
Rain letting up, clouds clearing out, and the sun shining through
I bounce back
Because I have to
Never will I lose sight of the primary objective
Make it home in one piece with a sound mind
I will soldier through any and every situation prison throws at me
And come out of here better than I came in
I just can't help but wonder
Was it a dropped call?
Then again, I know better

It's Such a Cold, Damp Day

Pain and struggle is all I know. A lifetime spent rebelling against an oppression that I can never seem to come close to entailing in its totality, nor do I feel I understand entirely. The only thing that I'm completely sure of is that my whole being, mind, body, and soul fights against this enigmatic force, which seems to have been woven into the very fabric of the consciousness of the people.

From birth, I've been looked upon with a mixture of love, hate, fear, and disdain. Stigma has cursed my very existence from the time I was able to walk to the corner store by myself. If the collective believes it so, then so it is, and I have not escaped its energy. In fact, I'm engulfed by it. Though I've managed to elevate my mind to heights I'd have never imagined, the taste is bittersweet because my environment and my daily experience fights relentlessly to purge my mind of its newly acquired knowledge. And at present, I have no way out. Thus, the struggle has been long, and I am tired--so tired.

If only I could get away from this wretched place that torments my very soul! This unnatural place that leaves me in isolation and disconnected from life! Haven't I the right to live, to govern my own life? I strive to be free from this misery! Yet it eats at my spirit like hungry termites. And I remain trapped. Yet still, I refuse to be counted amongst the broken men. I will not quit, I will not perish, and most of all, I will not fear.

I'm angry. An unwanted bitterness has slowly crept into my heart over the years, and I don't know how to rid myself of it. From time to time, it'll show its

The Struggle

ugly head in the form of a mild, but cold, outburst that startles even me. Not the outburst itself, but the awareness that I was barely able to stifle the icy, painful wrath that roars inside of me. The antagonist in me sneers at me and says, "You're losing this battle, and you have no recourse in sight." Perhaps. But I absolutely refuse to lose this war…

I suppose that some type of balance must exist in all things. With the gift comes the curse as well, and vice versa. It seems as if with all the pain and hurt that has come with my struggle also comes an incredible, almost uncanny self-awareness and sensitivity. A certain degree of enlightenment and clarity that gives me vision by which I guide my life. That, to me, is a blessing; a gift. One that doesn't, by any stretch of the imagination, come cheap. Talk about give and take! Still, I have an ocean of unshed tears that fill my soul. And at times, it seems as though it will pour over and never cease to flow. Here, the law of polarity is as clear as day to me. I'm one big walking contradiction.

A Song From A Caged Bird

I'm a caged bird eager to spread my wings
Ready to grace the world with such a beautiful thing
It seems my hopes and desires are simply dying
God gave me wings for a reason
I'm supposed to be flying
Flying high above the sky with the falcons and the eagles
Dapper in my brilliant attire so naturally regal
Exploring different corners and climates of this beautiful land
Where we took and ran with the message of "Yes, we can!"
Yes, I am a creation of the God supreme
He gives us permission and power
To chase our dreams, reach our goals
And watch as we reap what we sow
And with every accomplishment
My wings will continue to grow stronger, longer and better
With the wind as my friend
Prepped for any type of weather
Ready to begin a new journey, a new flight
Pushing the envelope for new struggles and new sights
Climbing up new heights

The Struggle

Just letting my star shine
Giving the glory to God
Because without Him, I would be left behind
My faith will carry me through this time of trouble and stressing
I'm destined to be an American Eagle
Soaring with God's blessings

Unconscious Tears

I've been carrying this load of incarceration for a very long time now, half my life. It's my burden to bear, and I own it. Day in and day out, I start my day with an unwavering faith in the unseen, an undying hope for a brighter future, deliberately guiding my thoughts in the direction of my heart's true desires. I long for freedom, love, romance, financial stability, in whatever way they manifest themselves, because I don't worry about the "how." Like my mother used to always say, "God works in mysterious ways" and "good things come to those who wait."

I've been waiting…

And just when I think I've conquered the beast, fought off all the demons, and resolved all of the trauma and issues that lay heavy on my soul, they regroup and attack. Thoughts and images so strong penetrate my mind—the pain so deep, and I cry unconscious tears. Still, until I'm able to lay down this load, until I'm able to heal from my many wounds, I will start each day with an unwavering faith in the unseen and undying hope for a brighter future, deliberately guiding my thoughts in the direction of my heart's true desire.

Expect the Unexpected

So, why shouldn't I do what's clearly expected of me?! Why shouldn't I sell crack in the hood to get money? That's expected of me! Why shouldn't I carry my .45, or keep my S.K. in the trunk? That's what's expected of me! Why shouldn't I be overly aggressive and smack the shit out of somebody as soon as they get me wrong in any way? Clearly, this is what they expect of me! Either I'm going to jail or I'm going to be killed, so why not embrace my destiny whole heartedly and go all out?

Hold on, hold on, wait a minute. Something's wrong with this train of thought. Maybe I'm moving a lil' too fast. Let me slow it down a bit, take a quick breather. Inhale… Exhale...

Okay, now let me re-evaluate this whole thing. I'm a direct descendent of kings; my blood line is rich and pure. Why shouldn't I conduct myself in a kingly maker? My ancestors are the parents of civilization. All nations of the earth sprang from the womb of my mother. Why shouldn't I be an example of excellence? I come from a people who're thirsty for knowledge and wisdom. Their understanding was matched by no other. Why should I break tradition? I'm a black man; The original man; The highest known form of manifestation; Made in God's own image. Shouldn't I act like it? It would be completely and totally uncharacteristic of me to ever allow the expectations of others to dictate my moves. I have God on my side. I cannot be destroyed, and I refuse to be defeated. My power knows no limits, and I intend to prove it. As the master of myself, and a free thinking individual, I wouldn't be me if I allowed others to determine my fate for me. The essence of my very being is divine greatness. I'm gonna be myself.

PART III
Reflections/ Introspection

Locked Up

All I've got are my dreams
All I've got are my visions
Trying to calculate ways to execute my own missions
Coming from a low place where stackin' bread was the issue
But if you get shot today, ain't nobody gonna miss you
My deep past in contrast to the things that I've learned
Got me focused on all of the strong bridges I've burned
Incarcerated, I'm pacin'--the tool I'm lackin' is patience
I need to slow it on down; instead, I'm actin' all anxious
Every day is a war--I'm fighting for self-preservation
In hopes that one day, it'll be the air of freedom I'm tastin'
Chasin' dreams, escaping reality when I can
All I've got is my pride—I will remain a man
Educating myself, slowly evicting my ignorance
If I've got a big problem, I break it down and I figure it
This here life is a lesson, a blessin' given from God
If I stumble and fall, I pick it up and restart
The library, my sanctuary with thousands of books
I keep reading when I'm receiving these venomous looks
From characters that think it's a game and ain't realized

Reflections/Introspection

I'm a man, there's no doubt when you look in these eyes
I rise to the test when cowards puff up their chest
Devour one and I'm sending a message to all of the rest
Avoiding conflicts ain't easy for convicts
When paranoia and stress is what causes this nonsense
The soul of a prison is power and control
I'm telling you people, really, it never grows old
Simply, the story is told bold, with truth as its essence
I'm only speakin' my truth but I hope you're feelin' my message

She

Survival is what she has given me all my life
She has kept me from feeling the hot hollow tips from my enemies' gun
Out of the blue, when everything seems normal
She would tell me, "I think we'd better go; something isn't right here"
I trust her, so we leave
No more than five minutes later
A blue Caprice pulls up and opens fire
Wounding two and killing two more
It could've been me
Insight, discernment and analysis are all her kindred
And they all show me favor
I depend on them
Living a thug life, they were the only friends I really had
But she can withstand the forces of lust, greed, and hunger for power
For only so long
They will soon prevail
She is good and comes from above
Continuing to undermine her gradually decreases her authority
Until eventually, her voice is just a faint whisper
And I no longer hear her

Reflections/Introspection

Without her, there's no balance and I slip
Some falls are harder than others
But every fall gets harder and harder
She wants me to listen and do good
She's my invisible but ever present helper
Everything is all good with her
Her name is Intuition

Silence is Golden

The mask I wear is one of silence. My mother used to always say that "we were created with one mouth and two ears for a reason, you should listen twice as much as you talk." I've always remembered that. She would tell my sister and me that just by listening to a person speak for a while, you would learn nearly everything you needed to know about that person. She said that a person who is talking 24/7 and never shuts up is most likely a liar, because there's not that much to talk about.

So I wear a mask of silence. Not necessarily because I have something to hide, but because I believe in discretion; everything isn't for everybody. A lot of the time, I don't have anything to say, so I say nothing. But I've come to realize that not everyone is as comfortable with silence as I am. As a matter of fact, silence makes some people very uncomfortable. I'm not sure why, but I notice it all the time. I guess different people have different reason; but something else my mother used to say is that people like to be able to place you in their own mental compartments of stereotypes or preconceived notions, but when a person is quiet, that makes it difficult for people to do this, and people fear what they don't know or can't conquer. So, I'm quite sure this has a whole lot to do with why a lot of people are uncomfortable with silence.

I'm cool with it either way, because what the ears can't catch, the eyes can. I'm not one to talk just to hear my own voice, or to make the next person feel at ease; it's a waste of time and energy. I'd much rather speak when I actually have something to say. If this is a mask, it has many more pros to wearing it than cons, so I'll continue to wear it.

My Homies, R.I.P.

You know, it's sad to acknowledge the fact that I was having trouble deciding on which one of my dead homies to write about. None of us should have that many options. So I decided to shoot all of them out.

Rest in peace Uncle Nose, who was one of the most giving people I knew.

Rest in peace Woop, who was a very mellow and laid back dude.

Rest in peace Dawan, who was one of the smoothest, coolest, flyest dudes I grew up with.

Rest in peace Big Paul, who stayed off the boat, but was a true hustler; he knew how to get money.

Rest in peace Timmy, who was known for his dirt bikes, pit bulls, and aggressive personality.

Rest in peace Lil' Bump, who also was a go-getter.

Rest in peace Debo, who was my close friend, and whose death affected me the most. Debo was 6 feet tall and strong as an ox. He was cut up like crazy, and very aggressive on top of that, so it's not hard to figure out how he got the nickname Debo. He was a quietly attentive type, partly because he was always on alert for his next move, being the stick-up kid he was, and partly because that's

My Homies, R.I.P.

naturally who he was: quiet, analytical, reserved, ambitious, strong-minded, sensitive, thoughtful, and very loyal.

Debo was my right hand man. We were together almost every day, including the day he was shot and killed. The night before, we were getting drunk and high, and he, all of a sudden, became really serious. He told me that I was like his brother, and that if and when anybody has a problem with me, they've got a problem with him, and that he loved me. All that guy-to-guy affection was extremely awkward for me, so I said something like "Yeah man, I feel the same way," then tried to jump right back into high, goofball mode. When I reflect on these memories, I always feel like Debo maybe felt his time was coming soon—he just didn't know exactly when.

Everyone I've mentioned with the exception of one was under the age of 21 when they were gunned down, and none of them truly deserved to die so young. I believe that given the right circumstances and an opportunity, my man, Debo, would have turned his life around, and so I choose to honor my friend by changing my own life and becoming the kind of man that he never got the chance to be.

Dignity

I want to live my life in a dignified manner

Elegant and respectable, discreet but detectable

Morals strong enough to contribute to society

Molding lives for the better

Still down to earth and as real as it gets

Without the poison of hypocrisy, double standards and double lives

I want to lead by example, learn and teach, encourage and influence

I've always been generally a loner, but I create my own social and personal circles

I would say that I want to be an upstanding citizen, but that sounds too PC

So, I'll say I want to be a dignified Black man

Fighting against stereotypes, and contributing to a new and improved hybrid culture

Tribal Ties

I belong to the tribe of urban nerds
Well-read, Hugo Boss, Foamposite-wearing, project-raised poets
And to the tribe of health and fitness consultants
We have hours on top of hours of burpies and push-ups
On rec yards all across the BOP
And to the tribe of Know Thy Self
When one has knowledge of himself
He or she is so much closer to understanding God
And the universe we dwell in

Empathy

Culturally, we could definitely use some lessons on empathy. A lot of the time, we're so quick to judge and/or dismiss other people's struggle without even making an honest attempt to see things from their perspective. Prime example: The Black Lives Matter movement. Black people have taken a stand, proclaiming that we're human beings deserving of any and all human rights, and despite all of the overwhelming and undeniable evidence of systematic oppression of black people, we still have people (way too many), who dismiss and disregard this national problem. These people refuse, for whatever reason, to be empathetic to their fellow men and women, and that's the reason we'll continue to see problems in this country.

When I think of empathy, I think of the African concept of Ubuntu. It says something to the effect of, "I am because you are." To me, this one phrase embodies the fact that everything and everyone in the universe are connected. So when someone does something, good or bad, it's a reflection of the community that person comes from. Which is a reflection of the larger society, which is a reflection of that state, and so forth and so on. So, from a more universal viewpoint, we all bear some responsibility for not only ourselves, but each other as well. Developing our ability and willingness to empathize with each other will allow peace to gradually come in and reign supreme. I believe that's all people really want at the end of the day.

On a more personal note, there's one time in particular that I can recall when someone empathized with me. I had just turned 17 and I'd just left DC Jail about two weeks earlier. Now I was leaving one of those jails in Montgomery

Empathy

County, MD, absolutely clueless as to where I was going or what lay ahead. Needless to say, I was lonely and afraid. When we arrived at the airport, we were turned over to the US Marshalls. There was one woman who was very nice to me. This was highly unusual considering all of my prior experience with the US marshals, going back and forth to court. If you as much as blink wrong, they'll kick your ass in the bull-pen. Anyways, she put my hand cuffs and shackles on loosely and then asked, "They aren't too tight, are they sweetie? Because I can loosen them." I told her they were okay.

The marshal got all of us on the plane and seated, and before we took off, she came by and asked, "You okay, honey?" I told her I was. She checked on me one more time during the flight. And then, periodically, as she was doing her rounds or taking someone to the bathroom, she would smile at me. I was on that plane for a few hours before I was transferred to another one. But I never forgot that marshal and her kindness towards me. I've played this back in my mind numerous times, and at some point, I realized that she wasn't being this nice to any of the other prisoners. As a matter of fact, she was barely speaking to anyone else unless it was necessary. This is when I also realize that she was empathizing with me. I was the only juvenile on the plane, and I probably looked as scared and lost as I felt. But her kind words and gestures meant more to me than she may ever know. Peace be upon her wherever she may be.

Crayons

I am the color of electricity
Seldom seen, but innately powerful
I am the color of stagnated dreams
Suspended in time, unfulfilled
I am the color of true transformation
The color of self determination
Whatever color self-pity is
I'm the opposite
I am the color of jewels
Like that diamond in the rough
I am the color of grace
Moving calmly and unafraid
I am the color of strength
Standing firmly on my square
The color of respect, courage, honor
When affronted by lesser individuals
I am the color of hope
The color of Martin Luther King's dream
The color of Malcolm X's resolve
The color of Noble Drew Ali's fight

Crayons

I am all colors
I am as colorless as the air we breath
I am the color of Judaism, Christianity and Islam
I am the color of peace

Redemption

Elevating to a higher consciousness, vibrating on a higher level, becoming more in tune with self is what I believe it takes to restore balance in one's life. Having a firm understanding of the 7 laws of Tehuti, AKA the 7 Universal Laws. Mentalism, correspondence, vibration, polarity, gender, rhythm and cause and effect. Once we understand these, we understand that there's really no such thing as coincidence, and that nothing ever happens by chance. There's a reaction for every action. We begin to realize that our personal realities are direct reflections of our inner thoughts, thus, we begin to take on a more proactive approach to life. Acknowledging and becoming aware of karma working in our lives. What goes around comes around, and what goes up must come down. I guess that's one way of looking at how I ended up in my current situation.

I've done a lot of dirt, honestly speaking, and karma has definitely caught up with me. She's been teaching me a lesson for the past eight years, schoolin' me in the areas of humility and empathy. Honor and respect. Communication and honesty. It took some time, but I'm finally starting to get the picture. Every day I wake up is another chance to redeem myself and balance out my karma. I try hard to always be aware of my every thought, understanding that my thoughts are conscious energy also and as soon as I think something it's automatically released into the ether. And they will not come back void. Everything begins with thought, so if I'm thinking good thoughts I'm doing good deed. Balancing my karma. Redeeming myself from all the hurt and pain I've caused others. Governing my life with the anicent Egyptian concept of maat, which signifies justice, truth and righteousness or correct action. Trying to ensure that the effects of my causes are always roling in a positive direction. So far, I feel like I'm on the right track.

Learning

Learning is the true purpose of life. It is the main purpose for which we all manifested into this physical form, to learn the lessons of which the plane of things made manifest has to offer.

> "Know thy self and then thou shalt know the
> universe and God." ~ Pythagoras

To me, this first comes with the understanding that everything and everyone is connected in some way, shape, form or fashion. We are more similar than we are different and when we see a trait or characteristic in another that we don't like, it's usually because we feel like we've just stepped in front of a mirror. I think when we develop this understanding (and it definitely takes some time to develop), it becomes easier for us to begin to forgive ourselves or others. Studying world history and having at least a basic understanding of major events from the past is important as well, because if we're consciously aware of the mistakes of the past and we've learned from them, then our future will be that much more promising. This goes for our personal histories too. We're supposed to learn and seek knowledge from the cradle to the grave, so the learning process never ends and I think that's the beauty of it. Expanding our minds is so fun and exciting, and we never have to stop!

Just The Simple Things

The experience was one to remember--Inside-Out Prison Exchange Program Graduation 2016. It was amazing. Everyone present--insiders, outsiders, and administration—was riding a vibe so high it equaled pure synergy. For two and a half hours, there were no convicts or inmates, no CO's or LT's. Nothing like that. All of those labels and barriers disappeared. For two and a half hours, I connected with moms, brothers and daughters. I hung out with husbands, wives, cousins, children and dads. We laughed together, cried together, and ate together.

I had the honor and pleasure of meeting the mom of my fellow teacher's aide, Harlee. Her mom, Ms. Jackie, was a total joy. So welcoming and elegant. I saw exactly where Harlee got it from. I chatted with them for a few minutes until it was time for everyone to take our seats for the ceremony to start.

All of the speakers were very genuine and heartfelt, but the highlight for me was a woman named Betsy Jividen. She is a re-entry coordinator who also happens to be a prosecutor. Her speech was profound to me in the way she made a very intentional effort to congratulate all the students. It was raw and sincere, and I deeply appreciated her for that. It's always weird to think of the fact that she's a prosecutor. However, she wasn't on this day. No labels. No stigmas. She was simply one of us. After the ceremony was over, we all started mingling again. A few of the other students introduced me to their parents and loved ones. Then since I didn't have any family there, I wandered off to the side of the room so as not to intrude on anyone uninvited. Harlee and Ms. Jackie were standing there.

Just The Simple Things

"It's kind of awkward standing in the mist of everybody with their families," I said as I approached them.

"Come here and stand next to me; you can be my adopted son for the day!" Ms. Jackie said, and with a big kool-aid smile on my face, I obeyed.

Harlee began telling her mom that I've shared some of my writing with her and how she thinks I'm really good. We talked about my appeal process in court, and they both wished me luck, which I truly appreciated. We explained to Ms. Jackie all the things we were doing with the inmate organization we were a part of called "The Council," and I could tell Ms. Jackie was impressed. We parted ways for a few minutes, and Harlee and Ms. Jackie chatted with other classmates and their families.

I went over to meet the husband of our professor, Delia. He was very pleasant, mild mannered and laid back. Delia, who was also a part of The Council, and an angel I might add, was charming as always. She and I talked about what was next on our really big agenda and how we were both excited to get right to it. Delia truly has a heart of gold. Her commitment to education, justice and equality is evident as soon as you meet her. It's powerful and inspiring. She's just amazing. After kicking it with Delia for a few minutes, I started making my way back over, towards Harlee and Ms. Jackie, in my slow, carefree manner.

Ms. Jackie spotted me, and with the same care and genuine acceptance, she said, "Come on back over here, my newly adopted son!" And, wearing the same Kool-aid smile from earlier that I couldn't hide even if I wanted to, I returned to my spot next to her. The three of us continued to talk. I spoke when necessary, and when I saw fit to chime in, but for the most part, I was completely content with simply standing there listening to and observing Harlee and Ms. Jackie. Listening to them speak, their tone of voice, the fluctuation therein, their laugh, mannerisms, the way they moved their hands, their nail polish, earrings, the way they crossed their legs, everything about their femininity to me was glowing like a full moon on a beautiful summer's night, and I basked in the light.

I got locked up and taken away from my mom when I was 16, then she passed away three years later. I've always felt kind of cheated by life in a way. My

Reflections/Introspection

mom and I were really close, and though they say all things happen for the greater good, a lot of the time, I feel like I was robbed of my full mother-son relationship. But the way Ms. Jackie embraced me whole heartedly, and enveloped me in all that motherly love, I'll never forget. I was moved more than she may ever know. Ms. Jackie was the embodiment of charm and grace, and Harlee was just as witty, engaging and beautiful as always. I was completely aware of the high degree of normalcy I was experiencing in each and every moment. I felt a sense of balance that I hadn't felt in a long time, and words can't express how appreciative I was. I remained with the two of them for the rest of the ceremony, and I wouldn't have preferred it any other way.

Observe, Don't Absorb

The first time I'd ever heard the terminology "Post Traumatic Slave Disorder" was several years ago when I read *The New Jim Crow* by Michelle Alexander. I came across the term, and before reading further, it already made perfect sense to me. Michelle Alexander went on to put it in a proper perspective. As I've studied and continue to study, I've concluded that here in the U.S., black people have never had time to heal from centuries of slavery and the continual state sponsored domestic terrorism and oppression. Black people have been in a constant state of defense as our bodies, minds and spirits have constantly been under attack. Some of us are so desensitized and brainwashed that we've forgotten that we were under attack. This is a direct result of Post Traumatic Slave Disorder.

We're bombarded daily with images of black people being violated, brutalized and murdered. Now, on one hand, people must be made aware of what's going on; that's the only way we can make a change. However, on the other hand, nothing is being done by our so-called leaders and policy makers to fix this national crisis. The unnecessary acts of violence by cowardly police officers and other spineless individuals is nothing new to anyone; it's not new, everyone knows what's going on at this point. So this causes me to wonder why news stations, and other forms of media, continue to show us these disturbing images. Our so-called leaders have made it clear that they have no intention of truly correcting the situation. They attempt to misdirect the people by continuing to talk about the training of officers when they know, like we know, that this thing has very little to do with training of officers and everything to do with

Reflections/Introspection

outright racism, subtle implicit bias stigmatization, and most importantly, birthright theft.

I've had the opportunity to read the United Nations Universal Declaration of Human Rights (1948) and The United Nations Declarion on the Rights of Indigenous Peoples (2006). Apparently, a whole bunch of countries, including the U.S., came together and agreed on a set of rights that every man and woman, by right of birth, is entitled to. But when we look at the policies and our condition over here in the States, it's clear that something is incredibly wrong. Americans are being violated across the board at an all-time high, but it seems like most people are unaware, or have just accepted it. I'm not sure. But I would really like to know why these international, legally binding documents don't apply to us?

I digress; let me get back on track. So what's the purpose of the media continuing to show us these disturbing images? There are probably many seemingly valid ways to answer this question. However, I'm convinced that it's psychological warfare. I say this because any time a black man, woman or child is gunned down or brutalized in some fashion by police, the media not only keeps showing it to us, they immediately go on a smear campaign against the victim, doing everything they can to dehumanize, criminalize, and vilify him. All the while, the killer remains the "accused" or "alleged" even after the whole world has seen, with their own eyes, that this person is indeed the perpetrator. It never fails; we see it over and over again. The killer may, or may not, get charged, and if he goes, he rarely ever gets indicted, and if he does happen to get indicted, he'll beat it in trial because the system is designed that way. Many times, over the years, watching these scenarios has left me stressed and depressed. Well, one day, I had an "aha" moment. My stressed and depressed reaction is the exact desired effect of the powers that be. If nothing is being done to correct it, why keep showing it? There has to be a reason. Anybody with a heart reacts similarly, but the trick is that when you're stressed and depressed, you're not thinking straight. When you're not thinking straight, it's extremely difficult to be proactive.

A lot of people just begin to accept these images as their reality and feel a sense of hopelessness and helplessness to do anything about it. Thus, the powers that be have accomplished their goal, and that's a battle lost for us. Something that

Observe, Don't Absorb

I've learned and practiced daily is the art of observing without absorbing. This is the ability to witness any situation, especially an emotionally charged one, without becoming emotional yourself. It's all about consciously directing and redirecting your flow of thoughts. We have the power to remain poised and peaceful by choosing the thoughts that will keep us in that state. Let me be clear though, I'm not saying that we shouldn't feel some type of way about our current conditions, what I'm saying is that we need to discipline ourselves so that we can take that energy and use it to change our conditions for the better.

It starts with self. Once we realize that we have power over our emotions and what we do with them, our healing process can begin. We must know our history as well, by way of independent study, so we can understand how and why we're in the position we're in. This is a very necessary part of our healing process. Once we do these things, we become much more effective in our effort to improve our conditions. We must be proactive. We have to stop begging or expecting help and cooperation from those who, for centuries now, have shown us that they don't care about our well-being. As a matter of fact, our studies show us that they actually benefit from our oppression. It's insane to keep expecting something different. Let's move on. It's time to elevate. We must be fearless, upright and independent. We must continue to strive and organize. Those who would rather just complain without putting in any work, need to be quiet. You're in the way.

On another note, as far as Trump winning the presidency, don't worry about it. I understand the anger and frustration everyone feels. Everything Trump stands for and represents is contrary to what America claims to be. But America has never been what it claims to be. Pay attention. When you consider this fact, it actually begins to make a whole lot of sense that a man such as Trump can become president. I'm going to let you in on a little secret. The true definition of the word "worry" is to create the very situation or circumstances that you don't want. Observe, don't absorb. Be proactive. Whenever I see those groups of my fellow freedom fighters disturbing and disrupting Trump's rallies and white supremacy gatherings, it makes me so proud; I can't help but smile.

I'm Muslim, which means that I have a universal approach to practicing Islam, and this allows me to see through all of the fog that separates us and connects with any like-minded person regardless of their skin color, geographical

Reflections/Introspection

location or religious school of thought. For those who may not know, Islam means peace, peace being the absence of chaos and confusion. One of the five divine principles that I strive daily to live in accordance with is freedom. I believe this is the main thing we're all fighting for in one way or another. In my studies, I've come to understand that in order for us to be free, we must allow others to do the same thing. So let Trump and his supporters have their rallies. Observe, don't absorb. All the time and energy spent disrupting rallies is valuable time and energy that could be used continuing to unify, organize and become stronger. So remain peaceful and be proactive. The change that we want is not going to come from the government, as I mentioned earlier. It's going to come from the people, from us.

The great thing about it all is that consciousness is rising. I can feel it and I can see it. I read about and hear mention of so many groups and organizations, and just extraordinary people doing amazing things to contribute to the uplifting of fallen humanity. This is only the beginning; we're just getting started. So to all my proactive brothers and sisters out there, remember! Observe, don't absorb. We must continue to be the change that we want to see in the world.

Royalty Redeemed

Forged in the heat of battle
I am a soldier
Yeah, they thought I'd die young
But I grew older
Everything they taught was a lie
They had me brainwashed
All this pain, I had to get high
But still remained lost
Leaving home, I had to be strapped
Because at the end of the night
It ain't no promise; I'll make it back
That's everyday
I began to learn not to fear death
I saw it so much
I really began to fear-less
Moving fast
And right in accordance with their plan
Unconscious
I awoke a prisoner of war
One declared on me long before I was ever born

Reflections/Introspection

Conscience rise

I know they wish for my demise

I'm up now

Elevating toward that which is Divine

I began to listen

Sixth and seventh senses activated

I see fruition

Focus

Stay the course

Freedom is pending

I harmonize with the Laws

Transcending

I arise from the dirt clean

Fully redeemed

I represent an uncommon breed

I am a king

Mastering the Pain

Feeling everything so deeply
Can be a gift and a curse
My happiness is true bliss
Everything just works
Suddenly, joy is replaced with pain
Clear skies fill up with rain
I try to hold on
But can't seem to maintain
My skies darken
Turmoil sets in
Damn
Never knew the mind could be like a wilderness one could be lost in
Lost many battles
Acting on impulse
Reacting with uncontrolled emotion
Never pausing to consider a reasonable course
I've felt the fire countless times
Intensified by a prison cell
12 by 9
A victim stance was my position
Playing the blame game

Reflections/Introspection

Meanwhile, in reality
My condition remained the same
Most of my lessons come the hard way
But were received nonetheless
My understanding is that much greater
I feel truly blessed
Being a thought of Allah made manifest
I consciously create
Striving every day to be the captain of this ship
The true master of my fate
The war is far from won
But my book is far from done
I have nothing to lose
But everything to gain
These first few chapters have been spent
Mastering the pain
Learning how to love
Breaking my mental chains
Rising above
This next section will be marked by liberty
I'll be free to pursue the queen that my heart desires
She'll be free to embrace our chemistry
Won't need a power of attorney
I can handle my affairs myself
I can eat life giving foods
That actually replenishes my health
No more limitations
Everything is possible
With discipline, persistence, patience
I overcome all obstacles

PART IV
The Light

My Roots

My roots began where all mankind began, on the great continent of Africa--North Africa to be more specific in my case. I'm a descendant of kings and queens, of high priests and priestesses, of men and women of natural medicine. My blood is that of ancient pharaohs and Carthaginian warriors. I have the vision and intellect of the great Moorish scholars, and the physical gracefulness of one naturally in tune with the rhythm of the universe.

My roots began in a time of matriarchal principles. A time when women ruled entire empires, and lineage was passed down through the mother. A time when women trained men in the use of weapons and war strategy, and fought right alongside their men. A time when a man didn't frown upon a desired woman who had already birthed a child, but he rejoiced in the fact, for it was proof that this desired woman was whole and fertile. A time when black African women were legendary for their power and beauty.

My roots began in a time when health consciousness wasn't just trendy. A time when people understood the importance of holistic health, mind, body, and spirit. They understood that we, as human beings, weren't actually designed to digest meat, and so the diet largely consisted of fruits, vegetables, grains, nuts, beans, and all else that comes from the earth that's good and eatable. Nearly everyone was physically lean and healthy, and lived much longer.

My roots began in a time when spirituality ruled over religion, and the word 'pagan' wasn't automatically associated with so many negative, misleading ideas. A time of gods and goddesses too. A time centuries before Judaism,

The Light

Christianity, and Islam. A place where mystery schools could be easily found all over. From Ancient Kemet to Ancient Briton, and all through Asia and the Americas as well. Universities existed where you thoroughly studied the 7 Liberal Arts: Arithmetic, Geometry, Rhetoric, Logic, Grammar, Music, and Astrology.

Knowledge of self was the ultimate objective. After all, we are the question and the answer. That's just a lil' glimpse at my roots.

Beauty in my Blackness

There is a beauty beneath my chocolate skin
True beauty is something that comes from within
Some of the most beautiful people do the ugliest things
Actions dictated by distorted beliefs and misguided dreams
Deep in the poverty stricken, drug infested, predominately Black inner cities of America
Is a very subtle beauty that only the keen and insightful can see
A rhythm, a universal style and creativity
An unyielding strength and perseverance of one nation
As controversial as it is, facts don't change
And stereotypes do us no favors, focusing on the negative at all times
I am automatically prejudged
When I pull up in my big SUV with 20 inch rims and tinted windows
People assume they know me
When I'm wearing my designer clothes, shoes and expensive jewelry
We are a proud people and have reason to be
Rap, Hip-hop and R&B are all criticized and looked down upon
Because of their brutally honest and explicit lyrics
A release of rage, pain and fury
Foreign to those who like to be judges of that which they are ignorant
Music that gives us hope and helps us see our way through an everlasting storm

The Light

Even if it is rebellious and extremely blunt
It's a guiding light for those in the most severe of situations
Every culture has its flaws in some way, shape, form or fashion
I come from a mighty, strong people
I find beauty in my Blackness

My World

I was born into a world where the only language men understand is violence and you have to be trained to go at the drop of a hat. Displaying physical aggression at any given moment. Gun, knife, or a bat, or hand to hand combat; you never knew. You just had to be ready to work with no hesitation.

A world where your reputation is everything; it can make or break you. A world where it's best to simply stay in your lane, play your role. Because when you try to step outside of yourself into someone else's position, it's only a matter of time before those that occupy that same position figure out that you don't belong there. Then exposure can, and will take place.

And in the world I was born into, exposure can be a matter of life and death... I was born into a world where there's no such a thing as meek; either you're strong or you're weak. Predator or prey. Any chance of finding a grey area is slim to none.

A world where manhood is defined by how many girls you can have sex with, how much money you have, and whether your guns goes off or not.

A world where extortions, armed robberies and drug dealings are a part of everyday activities, from sunup to sundown. A world where the probability of your death being a homicide is much higher... I was born into a world where most people who don't know how to cope with the pain of their struggle try to numb it with drugs and alcohol.

The Light

A world full of so much potential but the people have endured centuries of brain-washing that has taught them to hate themselves. The young man doesn't value his own life much at all, so he surely won't think twice about taking yours. The young woman will sell her body to you for a dime rock, a dippa or an E-Pill. How much value can she possibly be putting on herself?

A world where we're conditioned from early on to believe that somehow, being educated and well-spoken is lame and uncool. A world where the gentleman generally doesn't exist because we've been terribly misinformed, whether it was directly or indirectly, as to how we're supposed to treat women. I was born into a world where most never escape, and blessed are the few that do…

I was born into a world where it's not nearly as glamorous as mega-media would have you believe. It's an everyday struggle to simply survive. I just wish all of my brothers and sisters in the struggle the best. I would love to see my world rise above the current state of mind, back into our original state consciousness. I've highlighted the problems, but I choose to be a part of the solution. I will start by being the change I would like to see in the world. The more I learn, the more I will grow, the more I will rise and shine and be a source of light for others.

Justice for Trayvon - The George Zimmerman Trial

I have been following the George Zimmerman trial closely, and I must say, I'm not very impressed. I am very interested, but not impressed at all. I just can't seem to wrap my mind around how anyone could believe Zimmerman's claim of self-defense; it seems that there are many who believe and support him strongly. Even though I know and agree that we must get as close to the truth as possible, I feel like this man is given far too much leeway. Too many people are quick to believe his version of what happened but it's not that hard to figure out why he's wrong. And that troubles me.

Let's go over what we know about the situation. According to Zimmerman, he saw what he considered a "suspicious" individual that night. He called a non-emergency 911 number as he watched and followed Trayvon Martin in his car. During the conversation between Zimmerman and the dispatcher, he said that Trayvon took off running. At that point, Zimmerman got out of his car and started to follow Trayvon on foot. Evidently, the dispatcher heard the wind blowing through the phone and asked Zimmerman, "Are you following him?"

"Yeah," Zimmerman replied.

"Okay, we don't need you to do that."

"Okay," Zimmerman said. But we now know that Zimmerman did continue to pursue Trayvon. Zimmerman says that he lost sight of Trayvon, so he stopped following him and turned around to go back to his car. He said Trayvon jumped

The Light

out of the darkness and attacked him. This is where the story becomes foggy because it just doesn't make sense.

First of all, from the presented facts, Trayvon was trying to get away from Zimmerman at every point in the situation. That idea is consistent with Zimmerman's non-emergency 911 call and the testimony of Rachel Jeante, who was on the phone with Trayvon at the time. Also, it's a huge assumption to claim that Trayvon knew that Zimmerman was going to come after him when he started to run from Zimmerman. Why would he hide in the darkness with the intention to jump and attack a man he was clearly afraid of and trying to get away from?

When Rachel Jeantel got on the stand to tell what happened that night, her story remained consistent. Trayvon noticed this "creepy ass cracker" following him. He felt scared, ran, lost Zimmerman, and told Rachel what happened. She told him to run again but Trayvon refused since he was almost home. Instead, he started to walk quickly. Then seconds later, Trayvon says, "Oh shit! This nigga's right behind me!" At this time, Trayvon asked Zimmerman, "What're you following me for?" Then the altercation took place.

Who attacks someone, at the same time, trying to get away from him or her? Furthermore, who attacks someone while talking to a friend on the phone? It doesn't make sense. All of the facts, especially the 911 non-emergency call and Rachel Jeantel's phone call, tell me that Trayvon was scared, startled, frightened of this strange man who was following him.

Now that I've touched on Trayvon Martin's mental and emotional state during the minutes before his death, I would like to explore the mindset of George Zimmerman. It's been well established that Zimmerman irrationally viewed all young black men as threats, "suspicious," and "up to something." We know this because of the fact that he called the police 40 to 50 times in the months prior to Trayvon's death. Each call to the police was about young black men, with the exception of two or three.

Zimmerman's conversation with the dispatcher that night revealed comments like "these fucking assholes, they always get away," and "fucking coons." The people that controlled this part of the situation presented the statement as "fucking punks," changing it from the original phrase. Frankly, I don't care what word they changed it to because after listening to it numerous times, I still hear "fucking coons." Coons and punks sound nothing alike.

Let us not forget that early on in this case, Zimmerman's own cousin admitted that their family doesn't like black people unless they act white. With all this information about Zimmerman, it is clear to me that he was an angry, racist, wannabe-cop who decided he was going to take matters into his own hands.

Now, in all fairness, I'm not saying that Zimmerman intended to kill Trayvon; what I am saying is that Zimmerman was sick and tired of how "they always get away" and wasn't going to let it happen again. Zimmerman decided he was going to make an illegal citizen's arrest and perhaps hold Trayvon until the police got there; although it didn't go exactly how he saw it in his mind.

In the first week, there was a lot of focus put on who was on top during the fight between Zimmerman and Trayvon. This focus was most likely due to conflicting witness testimonies. However, I'd like to point out that only one witness stated that Trayvon was on top while four or five other witnesses claimed Zimmerman was on top. My question is what will this determine? It was a fight in wet grass! It's easy to conclude that they were both on top at some time point. That doesn't prove anything. Zimmerman felt powerful since he had a fully loaded handgun and had been trained in MMA fighting style for 18 months. He thought it would be easy to subdue little Trayvon until the police got there. But that's not how it happened.

Trayvon resisted, put up a fight, and defended himself. It's clear he did it far better than Zimmerman expected. Trayvon probably started to get the better of Zimmerman during the fight or Zimmerman just got angry at the scrawny, little, black boy who was giving him a run for his money. Either way, Zimmerman decided to shoot Trayvon.

This is my theory: when you take this 200+ pound, 29-year-old grown man with extensive MMA training and put him up against an average 15- pound 17-year-old boy, then can we really believe that Trayvon was beating Zimmerman to a point where Zimmerman honestly thought his life was in danger? Let's be real, let's be logical, and let's use our reasoning skills: It doesn't add up.

# The Light

There's so much about Zimmerman's story that makes no sense. Who gets shot through the heart and lungs and says, "Oh, you got me?" That doesn't happen. Why? Because you die after you sustain an injury like that. Zimmerman wanted us to believe that Trayvon said that right after he was shot. Zimmerman is lying though because the medical examiner said that Trayvon would not have been able to speak since the bullet hit him in the lungs.

Zimmerman also said that he spread Trayvon's arms out, after he killed him but when the police came to the scene, they found Trayvon with his arms under his body. The medical examiner did say during the cross examination, that Trayvon may have been able to move very little after he was shot since he could've lived anywhere from one to ten minutes. But let's remember that during the direct examination, the medical examiner said that it was his opinion that Trayvon wouldn't have been able to move. So when the medical examiner said that, Trayvon might have been capable of "very little movement," it probably meant only a twitch of the fingers or toes, not spreading your arms and tucking them under your body. It would take far more strength to do that after being shot through the heart and lungs. So I don't buy that story either; George Zimmerman is lying.

The other medical examiner, who treated Zimmerman's wounds, testified that his wounds were minor and superficial with only one, at most two, hits to the head, nowhere near the 25 to 30 times Zimmerman claimed.

Also, let's not forget that he said in a national interview that prior to this case, he had never even heard of the stand-your-ground law. However, his old college professor testified that Zimmerman took a criminal justice course, a course where he received an A. He admitted that although the textbook for the class did not specifically focus on Florida law nor used the specific term "stand-your-ground law," he still taught them about Florida's self-defense laws from his own knowledge. He said that the self-defense portion of the course was a topic that took time to learn and the class found interest in. He said that he continuously found himself repeating the portion of self-defense to his class.

To all of George Zimmerman's supporters, how many lies does this man have to tell before we start to question his credibility? Was it just me or did Zimmerman's uncle look so full of it up there on the stand? I won't even waste my time quoting anything out of his testimony because it was so ridiculous and shameful.

There's just so much that doesn't add up. Zimmerman told his friend that Trayvon grabbed the gun but Trayvon's DNA was never found on it. Zimmerman said that Trayvon covered Zimmerman's mouth and nose with his hand but there is no blood or DNA of Zimmerman found on Trayvon's hands. Zimmerman also said that Trayvon punched him in the face 25 to 30 times but again, no blood or DNA of Zimmerman was found on Trayvon's hands. Take it from one that has been in countless fights: if you hit someone in the face 25 to 30 times, some of their blood will be on your hands or you might cut your fist on their teeth. But Trayvon had no such cuts or bruises on his hands. News flash: George Zimmerman is lying.

For those that think that race had nothing to do with this, I would say that you're either in denial or simply naïve because this situation has race written all over it. If Trayvon were a white boy, he would've never been profiled, chased, and shot dead. If Zimmerman were black, he would've gotten 25 to life last year, and no one would've cared. We would know nothing about it. That's just the reality of it all. However, it's not over yet and I'll be tuning in until the end. Hopefully, by the time it's all said and done, justice will be served and the Martin family can finally have some closure.

The Verdict

I am enraged by the Trayvon Martin case! It infuriates me that in 2012, a white man can still murder a black teenage boy in cold blood and not be arrested and charged with the crime! Here, this white man is standing over the dead body of this black teenage boy when the police arrive on the scene and he just tells the police, "Oh, it was self-defense." And they're like, "Oh, alright. You have a good night sir." And this white man, this George Zimmerman walks away free as a bird. There's nothing right about this by any standards or any stretch of the imagination! We all know that had the roles been switched, the results of this situation would have been dramatically different! It becomes that much more clear and evident that this was murder when you start to add all the details to the situation. Now, everyone wants to shift the focus to the "stand your ground law" and make it an issue as to whether Zimmerman was legally in the right. This question, in itself, is an absolute insult for the obvious reasons! On top of that, the Sanford Police Department and other PD's across the country are now trying to pretend like it's so difficult to interpret and apply this law when the law is plainly written. But even if the law needs to be tweaked or erased, all of that isn't very relevant because even in its current form, it does not protect Zimmerman and does not apply to this case in any way, shape, form or fashion. A person with the lowest comprehension level can tell you this!

This thing is much bigger than some "stand your ground" law. Frankly, that's just a smoke screen to distract from the real issue. The way this incident played itself out, and is playing itself out, speaks volumes to the way young black men and boys are viewed and perceived in this country. This isn't anything new though. It's just that America wants to believe that we live in a post-racist

The Verdict

society and that all the ugliness is behind us. That simply just isn't reality. For many, many reasons, America has this deeply rooted fear of black men. One of the main reasons is how the media perpetuates stereotypes of us as the "violent criminal black man." The news is forever showing us getting locked up for one thing or another, or has our faces plastered over somebody's wanted poster. What makes it so crazy is the fact that whites get arrested just as much, if not more, than we do, but you hardly ever see them portrayed like they portray us. This fear of black men goes all the way back to the slavery era and is still showing up today. It seems as though White America is intimidated by the very presence of a black man. People fear what they don't understand and hate what they can't conquer. But we're the ones that should be scared! We're the ones continuously being murdered in cold blood by the very people who are supposed to be protecting and serving us! The very ones who are supposed to be enforcing law and order!

The evidence of this fear clearly presents itself within this situation. Nearly a month has passed and George Zimmerman is yet to be charged or arrested. As a result of this blatant disregard for law and grave injustice, the New Black Panther Party has issued a 10,000 dollar reward for the capture of George Zimmerman. The Black Panther Party plans to conduct a lawful citizen's arrest for the murder of Trayvon Martin, and they intend to hold him in custody until the authorities are ready to come get him and charge him officially. Immediately after the Black Panther Party revealed their intentions, the Sanford Police Department issued a statement saying something to the effect of "Let the police handle police business. We don't need any vigilantes doing anything to promote violence." Why didn't they tell George Zimmerman this when he was pursuing Trayvon Martin? When black men come together for any kind of cause, White America gets extremely nervous. But with all credit due to the police dispatcher, she did tell him "We don't need you to do that," when Zimmerman told her that he was following Trayvon. And her message shouldn't have had to have been much clearer. It was clear enough. So, what more is there to investigate? Everyone keeps talking about how a thorough investigation needs to be conducted so that all the facts of the case can be determined. But what else exactly needs to be known?! They have the murder weapon, they have eyewitnesses, and they even have ear witnesses! They have the confession for Christ's sake! What else is needed! I know too many black men in here with me who are doing life sentences, or 30 and 40 years, for crimes when there was

The Light

hardly any evidence to convict them whatsoever! Yet instead, they have everything they need to arrest, charge, indict, try and convict this white man but he walks free! And all the police have to say about it is that they know exactly where George Zimmerman is if they were to need him. That's how much they value the life of a black man.

This is not just a "black issue." This is an issue that we need to deal with as a whole. Not only are black parents suffering, we have a whole lot of white mothers who have black sons, and they too live in fear that any day, their child could leave the house and be gunned down simply because of the color of their skin. Something has got to give. The collective conscience of the people has got to change. When I use the words "White" and "White America," I'm only referring to Caucasian people in general, very loosely. More specifically, I'm speaking of that attitude, that disposition, that superiority complex! Though it's predominantly a Caucasian people thing, many minorities have a "White" state of mind as well.

It's a shame that we, as young black boys, have to have "the talk" with our parents at one point in time as we're growing up. As if we're the enemy! Oh yeah, my mother had "the talk" with me when I was about 12. We're taught to basically shrink up and tone down in the presence of the police. Don't move at all. Don't stare, keep your hands where they can see them, and don't reach for anything too quickly. Be very respectful, don't get loud, shrink your tone of voice and don't talk too much. This is generally what our parents teach us when they have "the talk" with us. And the authorities expect us to act in this way, whether they know it or not. If we don't, if we show any type of pride and dignity, their train of thought automatically goes to "Oh, I'll show you." And there's no telling what will happen then.

I'm lucky to still be living, I guess. During one incident, I was about 13. The police stopped me, saying that I fit the description of an armed robbery suspect. They asked me where I was coming from and where I was going. I answered them and then told them I hadn't robbed anybody and I tried to walk away. The two officers grabbed me, slammed me on the hood of the car and damn near broke my arm with some type of submission hold, where they take your arm and fold it behind your back and keep pushing upward. They didn't even arrest me or say anything about this alleged armed robbery they were

The Verdict

originally stopping me for. Once they'd had enough of seeing me in pain, they just let me go.

Another time when I was about 14, it happened again. Only difference this time was they jacked me up against a wall, slammed my head against it and choked me. Growing up, I didn't even think much of it because I was seeing this every day! And more often than not, my friends and others were getting much worse than me. We expected this. And they have the audacity to ask "If you didn't do nothing, why'd you run?" The nerve! Because I might be killed if I don't!

The Trayvon Martin Case is a tragedy, and I'm deeply disturbed because that could've easily been me. Trayvon Martin could've been my little brother. But I hope this situation is enough to spark the beginning of the change that we so desperately need. I truly hope so. One thing I am sure of though, is that until that change comes and when it arrives, I will be Black. I will not live in fear. I'm big, tall and powerfully built. My skin is dark and my voice is deep. I use strong body language when I'm speaking and I have a lot of tattoos. My hair is very nappy, as a matter of fact, I have dreads, and like Trayvon Martin, I like to wear hoodies too. I'm a black man and extremely proud of it.

Where Do We Go From Here? - A Tribute for Young Trayvon

Zimmerman's trial is over and he was found not guilty of all charges. With this verdict, a clear message was sent to black people across the country, that America doesn't value a black person's life--young black men's lives in particular. A white man can murder a young black boy, make up a bogus story of self-defense, have everyone believe it as 100% truth and not be held accountable in any way, shape, form or fashion. To keep it all the way real, it was a big "fuck you!" to every black person in America.

I'm angry, but not surprised. For one, when I found out that five out of the six jurors were going to be white--five southern, relatively older white women at that--I feared that they may have certain prejudices, or just straight-up racism that would strongly influence the way they viewed this case. I held on to hope though, throughout the trial. But when it was all over, the foundation of my fear was confirmed when juror B-37 gave an interview with CNN's Anderson Cooper.

Everything that came out of her mouth oozed with biased, prejudiced, pre-conceived notions. She said things like that Trayvon was responsible for his own death, and he should've run home. Zimmerman's version of the event was the truth to her. Evidently, she didn't care how many lies he'd been caught in. I found her interview to be ignorant and offensive, and I was disgusted by it. In the jurors' minds, Trayvon was every bit of the thug those defense attorneys and the media made him out to be from the beginning, even though there was nothing at all to prove that.

Where Do We Go From Here? - A Tribute for Young Trayvon

History teaches us that when it comes to the judicial system, African Americans are treated unfairly. Hold on, scratch that, because that's an understatement. We're the most hated when it comes to this broken judicial system. Blacks and whites get arrested at the same rate for everything, from parking tickets on up to capital murder, so how come we represent more than half the prison population in this country? Don't get me wrong, I've yet to meet an innocent man in prison, we've all done something to land us in here. But half of us have illegal sentences or have been railroaded in some way. Why haven't people stepped up to fight to make sure our constitutional rights are protected like they did for Zimmerman?

I followed the trial from start to finish on television, and I've been listening to a lot of the conversations that all the lawyers, legal analyst, experts and other people have been having. Something that stood out to me was how crazy the "stand your ground" law is. That was a big part of the problem in this case. I can pretty much start a fight with someone, and if I start losing that fight, I can murder that person and not even be arrested. That's crazy to me. Even though Zimmerman waived his right to an official "stand your ground" hearing, it was still put into the jury instructions for them to abide by. But this isn't even the main issue; it's much bigger than this.

A lot of the people on TV were fixated on this law, explaining their interpretations of it over and over, along with the fact that the prosecution has the burden of proof, they have to prove their case beyond a shadow of a doubt. The defense's job is to find or create reasonable doubt. From the jump, it didn't seem like a lot of the lawyers felt like the state had a strong case, and given the ins and outs of that self-defense law, I found myself reluctantly agreeing with them. It was impossible for the prosecution to prove their case because the one and only other eyewitness was the victim of this murder.

A lot of people have made it their business to point out that Zimmerman is Latino, not white. Okay, now we're talking about the main issue that influenced every aspect of this case and how it played itself out. Let's be perfectly clear though; his mother is Latina and his father is white. I would like to offer my thoughts on how the word "white" has evolved over the years, and try to give some context for people to understand how it's used a lot of the time. The word, white, is not always referring to one's skin color; it encompasses a hateful racist, prejudice, ignorant state of mind. It's a superiority complex, and one's skin doesn't have to be white to have these traits. So when we say "white people" this, and "white people" that, it's never an indictment on all Caucasian people, just those who fit the bill.

The other unspoken truth to this is that it applies to any and everybody, whether they be white, black, brown or yellow. And George Zimmerman is a racist "white" man. A lot of people also like to lean on the fact that the feds supposedly did an investigation into the case to determine whether, or not, race played a factor or not; coincidentally, that was around the same time that Zimmerman's words on his 911 call were changed from "fuckin coons" to "fuckin punks," so needless to say, the feds said that race was not a part of this case. The feds are the same ones that have countless black men locked up for make-believe drugs and make-believe guns.

It's ridiculous how many dudes I know that are in here for five or ten bricks of cocaine, but the reality is that they've never even seen one! Half the time, these dudes were caught with absolutely nothing, but are sitting on 20 and 30 years because someone said they did something. So I don't put any stock in what the feds have to say about this. But the verdict is in, and we can't change that; now the conversation has become where do we go from here? How do we learn and grow from this situation?

One of the problems with moving forward and learning from this is that so many people refuse to see this as a race issue. I'm not talking about the racist, prejudice, hateful people; they're going to believe what they want to believe, they're, to me, a lost cause. I'm talking about the people who know that Zimmerman was wrong in every way, the people who honestly want to see things get better in this country.

I'm not sure why it's so hard for so many to see what's so blatant. Maybe it's because the majority of those who feel this way aren't African American, so they can't understand, or maybe they simply don't want to acknowledge this harsh reality. I don't know. A lot of people have been saying that we should all care because this could've been anyone's child that was shot and killed in this way. Well, I only agree with half of that. Yes, we should all care about our youth as a nation, but this wouldn't have happened to just anyone's child, not in this way.

If Trayvon was a white child, he wouldn't have been racially profiled, stalked, and shot down like some wild animal; he would've been perfectly safe in that gated community. That's the harsh reality, and until everyone acknowledges that we can't move forward, then racial inequality will continue to fester in this country. I believe that a lot of people are prejudiced and bias subconsciously; they don't really know it. There are several situations I can think of off the top of the head. For example, a couple of years ago, Mel Gibson was recorded having a heated argument on the phone with his ex-girlfriend, and he told her that "I hope you get raped by a pack of wild niggers!" The dude who played Kramer on Seinfield was performing standup comedy at a club one night and apparently, some black guys were in the crowd heckling him. Well, Kramer went on an N-word rampage that night.

I'm sure most people are aware of celebrity chef Paula Dean's situation. She apparently has used the word, more often than not, out of pure ignorance. My point is, all it took was the right set of circumstances to present themselves and their racism, prejudice and bias all came flooding to the surface, and there's a chance that they didn't even know it was there in the first place.

My hope is that Trayvon Martin's story will be enough to wake people up to reality, especially after this verdict. I would ask all the people who agree with this verdict, but don't think they have any bias toward black people, to do some real soul searching and be completely honest with themselves about what type of thoughts and feelings come to them when they think about black people, especially young black men. We're not all bad, or thugs, or violent, no matter how the media likes to portray us.

For all the genuinely concerned people not to acknowledge that race played a major factor in this situation, as it does in so many situations, and not speak out against it, would be to silently condone these tragic injustices that just keep happening. More importantly though, we as black people have a responsibility to ourselves to become more proactive and much more engaged in local and national politics. Evidently, we've been way too relaxed, passive and reactive because every time we look up, some laws have been passed that either directly or indirectly work against us. Then when something horrible happens, we're standing around looking foolish because we didn't know.

It was so easy back in the 80's and into the 90's for Reagan/Clinton administrations to pass and hold on to certain laws that worked directly against us, like when they changed the cocaine and crack cocaine ratio to 100-to-1, meaning that you'd get 100 times more time in prison for crack than you'd get for cocaine. This was all a part of the so called "war on drugs" and everybody now agrees that these types of laws were racially discriminatory, and caused the high incarceration of black men we see now. It's been so easy for them to pass laws that allow young black and brown kids to be locked up, charged, and sentenced as adults as young as 14 years old in some states. All because we haven't been paying attention.

We've been clueless to what's been going on until it explodes in our faces. It's our responsibility to be involved with the making of the laws that govern us. We can change everything, we definitely have the numbers; we just have to remember that these politicians work for us. Democracy is a government for the people, by the people. All these demonstrations are good, we need to express our outrage at the continued injustices, but after we're done venting, we have to start playing this game the way it's supposed to be played.

Vote, attend town halls, address the city council and whoever else needs to be addressed. It would also be a real good look to have a whole lot more people in government who look like us, come from where we come from, and personally know our struggle to represent us and fight for equality. This is where we should start. And all of us Americans need to start talking more openly and honestly about race, because the reality of it is that this country is a melting pot.

We're all over here together, so if we could try to have more understanding about each other, then maybe we can harmonize. I wish everybody could be like Ms. Jenny Hutt. She's a beautiful woman who I have the biggest crush on right now; she often co-hosts with Dr. Drew on his HLN show, Dr. Drew On Call, and she just strikes me as a very pure soul. I've been watching Dr. Drew's show nearly every night, for the past several weeks, and I love mostly everything that Jenny Hutt says; all her comments on this trial, on race in America,

Where Do We Go From Here? - A Tribute for Young Trayvon

and on stuff just in general seem to come from a very logical, sensible, yet loving place.

At times though, I think her ability to see and focus on the good in all is so strong that it causes her to come across as somewhat naive. My point though, is that maybe it would help if we all just discarded everything we think we know about a particular group of people, and really take the time to learn about and understand others and their culture, then things would be so much smoother. Understanding is the key.

Rest in Peace Trayvon, and blessings be upon your loved ones.

What is Dead May Never Die

This past decade has been one full of collective and vicarious trauma, pain that I've had to experience from the most powerless position; in prison. Oscar Grant, Trayvon Martin, Mike Brown, Tamir Rice, Laquan Davis, Sandra Bland, Eric Garner, Philando Castile, Ahmaud Arbery, Breonna Taylor and many other individuals unnamed here, but definitely not forgotten. All of them killed by police or armed, privileged white men in cold blood. Most recently George Floyd was brutally murdered by police in a very similar fashion as Eric Garner. George Floyd struggled for air as he told the officer who had his knee pressed on his neck, "I can't breathe! I can't breathe!" That didn't matter in the past and it definitely didn't matter now. Nothing has changed, same old scene with the same old script and little variation. The first line the government always throws out there is something to the effect of "a full investigation will be conducted so that we can uncover all of the facts." But the facts are abundant and crystal clear at this point. Black people in general, but especially Black boys and men have been vilified, stigmatized, criminalized and dehumanized in every possible way in this country since 1555. This trauma, these impressions, are so deeply embedded in the subconscious of America that most people aren't even aware of their implicit biases.

Let me be clear, many if not most of these cases are the product of pure and straight up racism. However, it has become clear to me that a lot of these situations fall into the category of implicit biases, due to all the factors mentioned above that served the purpose of dehumanizing Black men in this society. Trayvon Martin was a case of racism through and through. Likewise, the recent situation involving a white woman walking her dog in Central Park threatening,

What is Dead May Never Die

out of pure hate, to call the police on a Black man with every intention of weaponizing law enforcement against him, potentially getting him murdered--that was pure racism.

Very often though, officers and other individuals involved in these murders and other miscarriages of justice are non-white. However, the common denominator in all of these cases is a dead or seriously injured Black man. These cases, continuously, one after the other over the years have played on my mind many a times as I considered my status and position in this world. As a Black man in prison I've experienced all sorts of verbal and non-verbal assassinations on my character from correctional officers and administrators and watched them physically abuse other incarcerated residents. I've been forced to endure some of the most inhumane living conditions. Imagine three grown men crammed in an 8x12 cell, only leaving it's confines for an hour a day, five days a week, living under the constant threat of serious injury or death. Then I turn on the TV or radio and hear stories and see images of Black people being portrayed in the most negative ways. The evening news shows us being terrorized and brutalized by the very people who have vowed to protect and serve.

The cumulative effect of it all can be devastating. However, I refuse to be defeated, I refuse to be broken. I will use my voice to speak up and speak out. Things won't change until laws are implemented that hold officers accountable in a meaningful way for their actions. Things won't change until we see more positive, uplifting, less stereo typical images of Black people on television. Things won't change until we educate ourselves *about* ourselves and truly implement the lessons we learn.

A big salute to all of the protesters who've been out there riding for George Floyd. They're going to hear us and feel us one way or the other. We can't stop until they do.

So Disrespectful

Terribly misinformed and misled by a subjective but collective train of thought that, after a while, surely became truth. "Fuck a bitch, duck a bitch, then leave a bitch alone." "We don't love these hoes." "I tell a bitch whatever she wanna hear, cuz I'm just tryna buss a nut." Thoughts such as these are predominant amongst many young men.

From the beginning, this perspective has had a dramatically negative effect on our interaction with the opposite sex. Somewhere along the line of history, the belief system toward women became, well, to put it bluntly, very hateful. We believe that women are beneath us, that we're somehow better than them, and that all they're good for is our sexual satisfaction. A lot of this is plainly evident in the double standards that exist. If a woman has multiple sex partners, she's a hoe. If a man has multiple sex partners, he's a playa. What's the difference? I haven't figured that out yet!

A lot of men feel like if their woman is unfaithful, there's no coming back from that, but if he's unfaithful, she's just supposed to forgive and forget. It doesn't make any sense to me. Some men even feel like they have the right to beat their girlfriend up "if she gets out of line." There's a total disregard for her being.

A guy and eight of his friends will get together and run a train on the girl around the corner and not think twice about it. Most times, this girl really does not want to do it, but these guys aren't conscious enough, or simply don't care about her social signals, her protest, and ultimately, how she feels. The irony of it all is that most of these same men love their mothers dearly and would see red if a dude even thought about treating her half as shitty as they treat other women. Most of these men don't seem to make that connection, and I was no exception. I was as guilty as everybody else.

Growing up, I had no male role model in my life; no one to teach and demonstrate to me what a real man is. I'm from the hood, so the examples I did have were the dudes on the block. Naturally, I followed suit, becoming a product of my environment. I was right in the mix, just as unconscious and uncaring as the rest. I think a lot of anger and/or disrespect men show toward women is directly related to a lack of understanding of their own emotion. We haven't been taught how to deal with feelings, how to acknowledge them, how to learn from them and proceed productively. In fact, we're taught the complete opposite.

When you start to show that you have feelings for a girl, you're teased for it. Called a "sucka for love," "soft," or "tender dick." It's needy; it's vulnerable; it's un-cool; it's emotional. And men don't deal in emotions. Instead, we suppress them and become walking bombs exploding in rage more often than not. Rage we know. We're very familiar with that feeling.

As a direct result of this blatant disrespect and disregard from guys, a lot of young women developed their own defenses and began to play the same game. "The only way he gonna get this pussy is if his money right." "The only reason I give him the time of day is because he bought this necklace, my car, and he pays my cell phone bill every month. If he wasn't doing none of that, he couldn't even talk to me." "Oh this dude is soft, and he likes me. All I gotta do is flirt with him a lil bit and I can work him every chance I get." It becomes a battle of the sexes but neither team wins. Everyone has guards up the size of the Great Wall of China! And both parties have a personal responsibility to take in the whole ordeal.

Men are like the sun, and women are like the moon; they complement each other, they need each other. Both have very important roles and responsibilities. The moon reflects the light of the sun. A wise man once told me that if a man is truly a man, and always striving to become better, then his household, all the way down to the dog, will follow his lead.

The Light

It has to start with us, the men. Once we realize that something is wrong, it's our responsibility to correct it. We must take the initiative and work toward becoming the best men we can be, giving a balanced amount of attention and energy to each aspect of our lives. Our women will reflect our light, and things will begin to harmonize much better. I believe that looking to the past will clear up a lot of confusion that exist these days as to what it really means to be a man. Civilization was much more spiritually and socially advanced in many ways. Everyone had a clear purpose and a role to fulfill in contribution to their family unit and community as a whole. The elders had specific ways of learning what each child's unique gifts and talents were, and each child was raised knowing, cultivating, and nurturing those gifts and talents in order to fulfill their purpose. In those times, there were certain customs and rituals a boy had to experience in order to transition from a child into manhood. He was taught how to treat a woman, how to pursue her, how to court her, how to love her. Amongst other things, no such customs and traditions exist today.

We're just free-styling, hoping that we got it right. That's why studying our history is so important; it has so much to offer us. There're a lot of boys running around perpetrating like they're men, when in all actuality, they're completely clueless. But we're not hopeless, we're far from that. Though it seems we've got a very long way to go, we have to start somewhere. Here's a good place to start; let's stop being so damn disrespectful!

Respect My "G"

I'll give my seat up to a lady on the train if it's crowded. When on a date with a young lady, I'm into opening the car door for her, pulling her chair out for her when we're about to dine, or giving her my jacket if it gets cold while we're perhaps taking a stroll in the park, acquainting ourselves with one another. I try to mind my manners and not use vulgar language in the presence of ladies…

Respect My Gentleman

I'm not really into turning the other cheek, and I take any and every threat seriously. Also, I don't make empty threats. I'm a firm believer in bringing my words to life. I will protect and defend myself and my loved ones. I'm forever processing and committing the patterns of men to memory, conscious of whom I'm surrounding myself with. The traits of men are a lot like the traits of animals in the jungle… no matter how hard you look, you will never see a lion and a hyena walking together in the jungle because the laws of nature won't allow it, and as a man, I try to abide by the same laws…

Respect My Gangsta'

I'm on my spiritual journey in search of spiritual enlightenment, trying to become more in tune with the self. I've begun practicing meditation, clearing my mind of everything, finding a slow, calm rhythm for my breathing, and simply being aware. I'm trying to get in the habit of always listening to my first mind, in any given situation. Always reminding myself that He is a part of me, and that I am a part of Him, so there are no limits. Ever…

Respect the God.

Death Before Dishonor

What is honor?
What is dishonor?
Because we really need to get this right
Is it honorable to kill a man
After you lose a fist fight?
Is it honorable to neglect your children
Thinking money makes it alright?
Is it honorable to beat a woman
When you're bigger and stronger
Or is it better to get away
Till your emotions are calmer?
Is it honorable to let your man "take the fall" for something you did
Then look down on a rat for snitchin' to avoid a bid?
Maybe I'm trippin'
Okay, cool
Maybe my logic is at fault
Two very different situations
But don't both end with the same result?
Is it honorable to leave a mess
Expecting someone else to clean it?

Death Before Dishonor

Is it honorable to stand on bold-faced lies
Knowing you don't really mean it?
Is it honorable to expect any person
To keep a standard that you know you can't hold?
Then turn around and judge that person
When they suddenly fold?
I could go on with relevant questions
That run through my head
For now, I'll leave you with just one
Why aren't we all dead?

We Need to Celebrate Our Achievements More!

We need to celebrate our achievements more often. And, we also need to continuously set new goals so we'll always be in a state of growth and development. If you're not growing, then you're surely dying.

I've achieved a few things over the years that I am proud of. I remember when I was in elementary school. I think I was in the second grade. My teacher, Ms. Abbott, got one of my poems published in a magazine. I remember being extremely proud and excited about that. Since I've been locked up, I've earned my High School Equivalency Diploma (HSED), a certificate in Institutional Food Production, another in Culinary Arts, and 17 college credits. I also received a certificate in carpentry. I once had the opportunity to write and direct a play for one of the prisons I've been in, and that was a lot of fun. It made me feel like I could perhaps, be a movie director one day. That same year, I was asked to write a song and perform for Christmas as well, and though I was super nervous up there in front of all those people, it was fun and I was proud of myself.

With all that said, I believe that my biggest achievement, and the one I'm most proud of, is self-transformation. When I was out there in the streets, I was crazy. Really insane! I continuously did things that were harmful to me and those around me. Probably the most extreme example I can use here is the fact that I used to smoke boat. Despite the strong probability that I would lunch out, which had happened multiple times before, I would still smoke it. One time, someone actually called the ambulance for me because I was trippin'. They had to literally force me down and strap me to a stretcher. I stayed in the hospital for about

We Need to Celebrate Our Achievements More!

five days before they let me out. And the very next day, I was smoking boat again. Insane. No exaggeration.

I've had the last nine years to reflect on my life, to practice introspection, and correct a lot of my old destructive thoughts and behaviors. But trust when I tell you I have a very long way to go, because I'm not there yet. I'm still a work in progress. But I feel as though it's been a great achievement to have made it this far, and I will continue to push forward as courageously as I began.

The Journey

I believe I've had many journeys already in this life, but none of them compare to the one I've been experiencing over the past five years. I mean, I was only 11 when I jumped off the porch and started hustling and robbing. So by the time I was 16, I had experienced a lot out there running the streets. At the same time, my life had not even begun yet. There are so many basic things that I haven't had the chance to do yet. And after you've been bidding for a while, you're always aware of how much the little things mean to you and how you miss them.

This whole nine years of incarceration has been a journey, but I put emphasis on the last five because even though my personal transformation began as soon as I got locked up, those first four years were a lil' rougher because I was still stuck in a lot of my old ways.

When I got shipped out in late 2003, I landed in a juvenile facility under contract with the Federal Bureau of Prisons. It was extremely strict, but I still managed to find trouble and self-destructive behaviors to get into. One day, out of nowhere, I was sitting in the hole when it struck me. Once you get past the mental and emotional toll of being confined in a tiny area for extended periods of time, it actually has a way of heightening your consciousness. I had this realization, with so much clarity-- I understood that it was *me*, and nobody else, that was causing so much confusion and disappointment in my life.

From that point forward, I've always made it my business to be completely aware of how all my decisions affect me, on a major and minor scale. I make it

The Journey

my business to have, at the very least, a passing knowledge of something before I choose to engage in it in any way. I no longer involve myself in self-destructive behaviors. I'm all about self-improvement. Every single day, in some small way, I'm always trying to be better than I was the previous day. I'm optimistic about what my future has in store for me because this journey is far from over. I know that as long as I continue north, I'll always be headed toward good things. And even if I stray away from the path, the good thing is that the path will be right there when I get back to it.

Victorious

I'm sittin' here chillin, thinkin'
About the past
All the stuff I've been through
Some thought I wouldn't last
I'm still standing
I've overcome many obstacles
I see success and I smell it all in my nostrils
It's mandated, this thing is like non-optional
Something to push against when these haters insist on knockin' you!
Aggressively pressin' forward
You can't ignore it
Finessin' you lyrically can't help but support it
I'm in a lane of my own and I can't be topped
I'm standin' firm like a pillar
And yes, I'm as strong as an ox
So versatile that I can't be stuffed in a box
My views are universal, no longer left in the dark
Can't be afraid or timid
Gotta be sure, keep raisin' the bar
Because I know I'm deserving of more

Victorious

I'ma keep on knockin'
Until they open the door and see what's arrived
Watch their chins drop to the floor
Yeah, I made it, endured what you could bring
I'm tested and tried, so give me my champion's ring
I dare to dream so I see the best is yet to come.
I'm about to rise, and shine, just like the sun
Never been one to run from a battle
I hold it down
Toe to toe, blow for blow, and round for round
Divinely inspired, I'm destined for greatness indeed
If you can't seem to find the way, just follow my lead
I'm on top, give me my props, and homie stand down
In case you don't notice partner, I'm the man now

Destiny Is Here

I've pushed through the dense trees and thick wet fog
Of the wilderness called the federal prison system
Fending off attacks on my sanity, my masculinity and person
Fifteen years has brought me full circle
Back to DC
My place of birth
My home
I've paid the price of redemption
Cultivated my mind with seeds of prosperity
And some have blossomed
Some have not yet bloomed
Still, destiny is here
And I'm only just getting started

PART V

Love

Big Homie

The big homie is patient and observant. He weighs situations and knows when to extend himself and when not to.

The big homie is a student of history. He's fully aware of, and understands the struggle that we, as brown-skinned people, continue to endure, and always considers this when dealing with his younger brothers and sisters.

The big homie is aware of the fact that through generations of slavery, we were trained to hate ourselves, and that this is a large part of the reason that we have so much crime, violence and malice within our communities. Therefore, he would never make statements like, "I can't stand these young niggaz these days!" or "These youngin's are fucked up these days." He understands that the young ones are an extension of the ones that came before them, so we are all responsible for our present condition.

The big homie studies economics. He passes this information on to his younger brothers and sisters, encouraging entrepreneurship and ownership, because he knows that financial freedom is the order of the day.

The big homie teaches the lil' homie that family is extremely important, because the family becomes the clan, the clan becomes the tribe, and the tribe becomes the nation.

The big homie teaches the lil' homies that he is the leader of his household. That he must be upright, fearless, and independent. That he must be a thinker and that the faculty of reason must be his constant companion.

Love

The big homie teaches the lil' homies that his body is a gift, a vehicle given to him to express himself in this realm of things made manifest. Therefore, he must keep it strong with physical activities, and clean with soap and water daily.

The big homie teaches the lil' homie that women are his other half, to be respected, cherished and protected. The big homie teaches the lil' homies that women are emotional by nature, but that it is his duty to support her through the strong emotions she experiences, and not to adopt the same reactive behaviors she exhibits at times.

The big homie teaches the lil' homies that with a woman's emotions come a powerful intuition, and when he has found himself a good woman, he'd be wise to heed that intuition.

The big homie doesn't let the thoughts and actions of others dictate the way he moves. When the lil' homies fail to listen and act accordingly, he doesn't give up on them, deeming them a lost cause. He continues to lead by example, knowing that he himself can't reach everyone, and that everyone doesn't wake up at the same time. However, he continues to be the change he'd like to see in the world.

The big homie is constantly working to improve himself because he understands that acquiring knowledge of self is a lifelong process, and that we must seek this knowledge from the cradle to the grave.

The big homie knows he must remain humble because he is aware of the fact that knowledge and wisdom can come from anywhere, anytime and anyone. Even someone younger than himself. Younger in age does not always equal younger in knowledge and wisdom. So, the big homie knows he must keep his ego in check.

If your big homie isn't teaching you any of these things, then he isn't a big homie at all. He's just a lil' nigga that's older than you.

A Vision

In my dreams, I see a family of seven
Me, my wife and the kids—three boys and two girls
Nothing's perfect, but we make due
Because I'm a man with a vision
Though there are bumps in the road
I follow through with precision
My wife is very supportive—yeah, we argue and fuss
But at the end of the day, our foundation is trust
We're soul mates at the raw and true essence of the word
Anything coming between us, well, that's kinda absurd
All of my children are individuals
I pay very close attention
I want them to be successful and so far, I think they're winning
My oldest son, Malachi, is very analytical
Always deep in thought, trying to find the subliminal
So we encourage him to debate and play chess
Read a good book when he needs to relieve stress
Giovanni and Lafayette are both musical talents
Lafayette writes rhymes while Giovanni sings ballads
We frequent the studio whenever I can give them the time

Love

Because I am also on a musical grind
Dakota's a beauty queen
She's all about fashion
She can't resist letting you know if your shoes and outfit aren't matching
I encourage her all the time
I never have to remind her
My baby girl knows she's gonna be a fashion designer
Kahleel, well, he's a little aggressive
I had to figure something out before his butt got arrested
He's taken up martial arts and it relieves a lot of his tension
It sure beats him being in after school detention
So far so good, I'm satisfied with my life
An accomplished music producer, with a beautiful teacher as my wife
I thank the Man up above for blessing me, time and time again
Even when I was sure I'd lose
He knew from the jump that I'd win

Uncharted Waters

I'm not sure I know what being in love is. I'm sure I've never been in love. I know this because the people I know that have, say that there's no mistaking it. "You just know" is what they say. Malcolm X says, "Love transcends just the physical. Love is disposition, behavior, attitude, thoughts, likes, dislikes – these things make a beautiful woman a beautiful wife. This is the beauty that never fades. Thus, we should look into our women for these things, and they into us." And if there's any truth to these words, which I believe there is, then there's 2 young ladies that I love right now. But I'm not in love with them. I like to think that the word "love" is an action verb, and I suppose that's why Malcolm X's words sit with me so well; because that's exactly what I've been thinking for the longest time.

Even with all that said, sometimes, I still have my doubts. I mean, the word love is filled with so much mystery. It seems to be a very complex emotion. How is one to be sure when they're feeling this "love"? And I'm assuming, perhaps wrongfully so, that the love I speak of is somehow different from the love one feels for their parents or siblings. This love I speak of is in a love all by itself; some statue perhaps, but of a different degree. In the smoldering heat of passion and desire, how does one find that blurry, nearly invisible line that separates love from lust? In the icy, freezing coldness of isolation, how does one differentiate between love and loneliness? Love and infatuation? This would be the root of my personal dilemma, and my lack of experience leaves me terribly confused and ill-equipped to navigate these foreign waters...

Love

Is there such a thing as love at first sight? Just because you love someone, does that mean you're supposed to be with them? They say we all have a soul mate out there, but are we limited to only one? Are we only supposed to be with and mate with one person our whole life? This last question I'm pretty sure I know the answer to, and some of the others are probably a little premature for me because I haven't had any experience. These are just some of the questions that arise when the subject of love comes up. I have theories for days, but my lack of experience with women in serious intimate relationships leaves me unsure about any of it. I'm 25 years old. I've been in prison since I was 16. What should I expect? What will be expected of me? Will I be able to meet these expectations? Am I too emotionally detached and/or screwed up to participate in a meaningful relationship? I'm nervous, maybe even a little scared. But I'm extremely excited as well. Excited to have the chance to live. Excited to have the chance to dive out the window and make mistakes. Love; Hurt; Love again; Hurt some more. Excited simply to be free to feel again. Over the years, I've suppressed so much that, more often than not, I'm just indifferent. When I do start to feel, because of the environment I'm forced to be in, I automatically suppress it. Which I know is not a good look at all. Though, like most people, I fear the unknown. I'm looking forward to loving and loving hard when my time comes. I mean, is there any other way?

In Her Eyes

I see the potential for forever
Subtle glimpses of lifetimes spent together
I see the heart of a mother
Tempered with the mind of a queen
I see an intelligent, competent conscious woman
Made for nothing less than a king
Strength and vulnerability are also there
Along with passion and compassion
And if I happen to be the vaguest question
She's the specified answer
I see a deep ocean full of love
That's barely been touched
And I just want to go deep sea diving
Giving her all of me
In exchange for us
Her beauty goes without saying
My soul yearns for more
Her eyes tell me likewise
And my soul is assured
I see the potential of forever

Love

But if we ever part ways
I'll always remember the power and potential
That live in her gaze

A Familiar Soul

As soon as you meet one another
There's not even the shadow of a doubt
That the encounter was meant to be
It's as if the universe stops
Just for a moment
To acknowledge this union
And cast a warm smile upon
A small portion of destiny realized
And you both feel it in your core
Your eyes connect with one another
And instantly, you feel this sense of peace,
Comfort, and safety
Flashes of intuition bring forth images
Of the two of you in your mind's eye
And you not only know this person
You know her intimately
You understand him deeply
And you know that the connection
That the two of you share
Is so deeply rooted in the cosmos

Love

That this couldn't just be
A figment of your imagination
And as your eyes meet once again
You've never been more sure of
Anything else in your life

Women

A woman is the vessel through which Allah saw fit to bring humanity into existence. How could her value ever be questioned? She is the nurturer, the caregiver, the governor of her household. She is a natural clairvoyant, always paying close attention to the seemingly unimportant details, able to effortlessly anticipate your needs and wants. The virtuous woman is a leader and counselor. With her warm affection, charm and grace, she easily coaxes you in the right direction.

The woman was created with full autonomy. She has the unabridged, natural right to make any and all decisions as it pertains to her property, her degree of education, her husband and her body. She is undoubtedly more than capable.

It has been argued, and accepted to a large degree, that women are too emotional, which makes them unfit for certain position of leadership. However, this argument is faulty. It suggests that logic and intellect are the only attributes required to make sound decisions, completely ignoring the Universal Law of Polarity and Balance. Could this be the reason we see so much imbalance in the world? Logic must be tempered with empathy. Intellect must be tempered with understanding. This is the only way true justice can be achieved. We would do well to heed the lessons of ancient civilizations where they showed great respect for the principle of equality between men and women. In ancient Kemet (Egypt), the role of the woman was not only respected and honored, but required and necessary throughout every facet of society. Still is, and always will be.

Hope

"Keep hope alive" is a phrase that most of us are familiar with, and no matter how cliché it is, it would be in all of our best interest to heed to this statement. When hope dies, so does humanity. When hope dies, so does empathy. When hope dies, so does compassion. Hope is one of the most powerful driving forces; when everything in our lives seems to have gone to waste, and options seem extremely limited, it is hope for the better that strengthens our will to make a way out of no way. Hope turns into faith, faith turns into action, and action equals fruition. Simple mathematics, but profound as well, to come into the understanding of how much power we actually have when we exercise the strength of the will, especially when we do so within the bounds of righteousness. Hope is what enables a person to rise up from the dirt to improve their conditions. Hope is what drives the well-off individual to reach out and assist the downtrodden in his or her efforts to improve their conditions. So it is our spiritual responsibility, individually and collectively, to "keep hope alive," because it truly makes the world a better place.

Missin' You
For Debo

You were my right hand man
At first, I couldn't understand
After a while, I had to let the tears burst
I felt cursed
Because we used to roll together
We balled together
We always stood tall together
And now, you're gone
And I understand where we went wrong
We leaned toward the wrong direction
Now I'm singin' this song
Ya' dead wrong
If ya' think I can't feel your pain
I'm steady in this game
But sometimes, I feel insane
I miss ya' man
And always know that you were the best
I always wondered why those bullets had to put you to rest
Two to the chest, three to the belly
I was so weak

Love

Standing there watchin' you bleed
I could barely speak
It's been three years
But you know, I don't wonder no more
Things have changed
And God already ordained
I'm resting in peace, 'cuz I know we'll meet again
Far as I know, we were both God's children
One love
R.I.P.

Her Embrace

It's like the world stops
Nothing exists but her and I
In these moments, nothing matters
But her slim, brown arms around my shoulders
My arms around her waist
The feel and scent of her breath
As our bodies press together for several intimate seconds
She smiles
I smile back
And the respect and admiration we hold for one another is evident
Her beautiful, brown eyes hold me captive in this moment
As a thousand manifestations of the potential I see in them flash in my mind
The universe has seen fit
To repeatedly bring her and I into each other's life experience
To share in this most common of human gestures
For most, this may seem minute and unimportant
However, to a man who has had everything taken from him
Deprived and denied by those who deem him less than a human being
This seemingly small gesture is life giving
Though I wish I could hold her longer, we part

Love

The world begins to move again
My spirit is restored for a time
And all it took was the gift of her hug

About the Author

Jonas Gilham is a writer and student at Georgetown University Prison Scholars Program. His writing has been published by *Dragonfly Arts Magazine*. He is the facilitator of Healthy Masculinity, a course for individuals incarcerated at the DC Jail. He was born and raised in Washington, DC.

Made in the USA
Middletown, DE
16 November 2024

64146171R00071